The Missing Link

Poems & Short Stories

The Missing Link

Poems & Short Stories

by

Telly Orekavala

Nenge Books

The Missing Link - Poems & Short Stories
by Telly Orekavala

Copyright © Telly Orekavala 2022

Cover illustration © Essy Junior Orekavala 2022

All rights reserved

This book or parts thereof may not be reproduced in any form, stored in a retrieval system, or transmitted in any form by any means - electronic, mechanical, photocopy, recording, or otherwise - without prior written permission of the publisher.

Published by Nenge Books, Australia, January 2023
ABN 26809396184
nengebooks1@gmail.com
www.nengebooks.com

Editing, layout and desktop by Nenge Books.

Nenge Books assists independent authors to publish quality ebooks and books using print-on-demand technology.

Scripture taken from the New King James Version®. Copyright © 1982 by Thomas Nelson. Used by permission. All rights reserved.

Scripture quotations marked (NIV) are taken from the Holy Bible, New International Version®, NIV®. Copyright © 1973, 1978, 1984, 2011 by Biblica, Inc.™ Used by permission of Zondervan. All rights reserved worldwide. www.zondervan.com. The "NIV" and "New International Version" are trademarks registered in the United States Patent and Trademark Office by Biblica, Inc.™

Also available as an ebook ISBN 978-0-6456758-2-5.

ISBN 978-0-6456758-3-2

"A musician must make music, an artist must paint, a poet must write, if he is to be ultimately at peace with himself. What a man can be, he must be."[1]

Abraham H. Maslow

"The purpose of a writer is to keep civilization from destroying itself."

Albert Camus

"Books! I dunno if ever I told you this, but books are the greatest gift one person can give another."

Bono

"There are books of which the backs and covers are by far the best parts." [2]

Charles Dickens

"Read a thousand books and your words will flow like a river." [3]

Virginia Woolf

---

1. Maslow, A. H. (1954). Motivation and personality (First ed.). Harper & Row. p.93
2. A quotation from Oliver Twist (Chapter 14). Oliver Twist, subtitled The Parish Boy's Progress, is the second novel by Charles Dickens, published in 1837.
3. Unable to trace source references for the other quotes on this page.

Dedication

The book is dedicated to my wife Christine Orekavala, children Essy Junior Orekavala, Nathan Orekavala, Salonda Orekavala, Isaac Orekavala and Rocelynda Orekavala.

Contents

Acknowledgements	ix
SHORT STORIES	
The Missing Link	1
Reward for Breaking the Silence	5
Grandma's K20 Coins	7
The Tool that Became a Weapon	9
My Papa and Mama's Bank	11
The Invisible Barrier	14
When Uncles Were a Step Ahead of Grandmother	16
I am Missing Something	18
The Runaway Priest	24
The Slain Opportunity	27
A Mother's Quest for Education	32
The Three Months Old Message	37
Mama Won Twice	40
A Kid's Definition of Alcohol	43
When the Hunted Became the Hunter	46
I Want to See It	48
POEMS	
Sonoma Race - 2016 November	52
Gone are the Days	53
What Meets the Eye is Deceptive	54
The Other Side of the Day	56
Father's Death	56
Be free bury the past	58

Black But Beautiful	59
No Real Black Man	60
The Thief	60
The New Moon	61
Malaria Attack	61
Widening Gap	62
I'd Rather Shut My Mouth	63
Blame or Accept	64
All in One, One in All	65
Who Cares?	65
The Dotted Sky	66
The Provoking Insect	67
The Hunter's Wish	68
Sacred Exposed	69
Light as a feather	70
He is Coming Soon	71
God Created the Sun	72
Time	73
Mama's Silent Tears	74
Love Thief	76
The Lost Fisherman's Fear	77
No One is Listening	78
My Lae	80
Comrades	81

Acknowledgements

The success of this book is attributed first of all to God the Father for the strength He gives me to accomplish any given task.

Philippians 4:13. (NKJV) *"I can do all things through Christ who strengthens me."*

I would like to also thank Ms Alphones Huvi. I wouldn't have attempted anything in writing if it wasn't through you. God brought you to me so that I can realize my potential.

Telly Orekavala
Buka, AROB, PNG
October 2022

The Missing Link

This is a true story of two sisters' search for Parental Love and Care.

Not every child born to couples in this country is lucky enough to be surrounded by parental love and care, their right to unconditional love. When the family is intact, children enjoy peace, happiness and the security they deserve, but when the opposite happens life becomes tough, leaving them with no other option but to fend for themselves - to live at all costs, even giving up their own lives.

This is a true story of two girls who went looking for the parental love and care that they rightly deserved but instead got caught up in all the adversities, glitches and negligence of life.

While on their endless search for love and care they confronted the realities of life, unwittingly entering the "School of Hard Knocks." They fled these predicaments from province to province for more than half a decade. Eventually, in 2011, they caught up with their run-away mum, but she was not the mother they once had or had expected to see. She had become insane due to the depression she suffered from her break up and the pain of losing her children.

Jenny (not her real name) and her siblings were brought up in a well-to-do family where the father had a well-paid job with a company in Port Moresby, and their mother did some clerical jobs. Both parents come from the Momase region but from different provinces.

Due to the nature of his work, the father was away on company errands most of the time. Because of the frequency of his travels, he started to neglect his family. This continued for some time, which placed increasing stress upon the mother as she could not afford to look after her kids in a big city like Port Moresby. Feeling that this would last forever, she prematurely ended the marriage in 2003 when Jenny was eleven years old.

She ran away with her nine-year-old son leaving the two girls, eleven and thirteen, with their father's relatives. That was the last time they saw her and they never heard anything from her from the day she left.

Life became harder for the pair. Later that year, 2003, they left Port Moresby for Lae in search of their mother, using plane tickets purchased by a sympathetic relative. They knew their mother was there as she was a Morobean.

After a year had gone by, life became even harder for the girls, living with paternal relatives at Lae's Bumbu settlement. Money sent to them by the father through the relatives never reached them. The father, having learnt of this, stopped sending money. He even kept changing his Bmobile SIM cards every now and then to avoid his relatives, who were feeding off him. But he still managed to maintain contact with his daughters.

Jenny thought life would be better if she lived with her grandparents. In 2005 she went to East Sepik province where her dad came from, with one of her aunts. To Jenny, it was a wonderful thing to be with her grandparents. She was happy that she could live with this caring aging couple.

Jenny's sister Judith, upon learning that her sister was doing fine in the village, followed a few months later as she couldn't live without her younger sister. The sisters reunited at their grandparents. What a joy it was for them to be together again and where Jenny eventually started attending primary school.

This provided an opportunity where they could care for their aging grandparents in return for the love and care they missed from their biological parents. The grandparents appreciated the treatment given by their granddaughters, long missed from their grown-up sons and daughters. They filled the vacuum created by the absence of their aunties and uncles. The old man had a dreadful skin disease while the grandmother was asthmatic.

They were a perfect team; the quartet turned to each other for help and comfort in times of need until their dear grandmother passed away in September 2009. A week later their grandfather also died, leaving them in the care of other relatives. This was a double blow which the girls were not prepared to accept. They were devastated.

Life after their grandparent's death became gloomier. Their previous life of sunshine suddenly turned cloudy and stormy clouds began to form. The husband of the aunt who brought Jenny to the village filled the shoes of their grandparents, but it was not to last. They were supposed to take care of them, but love was replaced with harshness and vulgarity.

Often, they were severely punished for trivial things. He even asked to marry Judith (not her real name) and when she refused, threatened to kill her. Life was so stressful living in this environment. So they decided to break free from this situation.

The sisters caught some fish and left their village to go to the nearest town to sell and raise some money. While there, a kind-hearted primary school teacher heard of their plight and promised to help them.

After making enough money from the sale of the fish, they travelled by PMV to Wewak, the provincial capital, accompanied by a cousin brother. Not long afterwards the female teacher lent them some money with a loan from Teachers Savings and Loan Society (TSL) and they paid for two tickets to Lae by ship.

Back in Lae the sisters were once again faced with the same dilemma. This time it was much worse than before. Judith couldn't stand it, so she fled the house and took refuge somewhere in the city.

There was no concern from the relatives, and no one bothered searching for her except for her soul sister Jenny. Her life without Judith was so miserable and lonely. But despite all, Jenny was a strong young woman who did not allow the situation to snatch life away from her. She continued to attend classes and was so determined to see her sister again. Her marks in school started dropping. She seemed to stay calm and nobody knew about her predicament. Wearing a fake smile but inside she carried an incinerating wound slowly bleeding her to death.

Whenever Jenny found time she would go looking for her sister. Her dream of meeting her sister paid off when at last, with the help of sympathetic wantoks, she found her sister. She left her aunt's house and went to live with her sister, but it was not to her aunt's liking. This added fuel to the fire. Her aunt threw Jenny's few belongings out of the house and told her to pack up and leave.

Jenny had no other choice but to take up residency with her sister at their wantok's house. This too did not go well and instead accentuated the problem. In all this turmoil the sisters' love for each other grew strong and they promised not to part from each other. They were indeed sisters in arms.

Judith decided to get married in 2010 so that they could find love and care, protected by walls of a home, which they had missed over the years. Above all it was to support Jenny with school fees so she could be able to complete her education.

Some months after her sister's marriage Jenny found her maternal uncle at Lae's main market. She embraced him, burst into tears and wept openly, reliving the pain she was carrying around. She was taken home to Manga, her mum's village in the Buang LLG of Bulolo district.

She continued her education in 2011, there never more to roam. And it is here that I caught up with her. She exclaimed she was in her mother's pouch, free from all her worries and problems. She completed her primary and secondary schooling in Morobe.

Today she is a happy young woman working at the Vision City, in Port Moresby. Since then, she has reunited with her dad and goes to work from there.

For her sister Judith, she got married to a man from Milne Bay, had children and lives in Lae, Morobe Province.

Reward for Breaking the Silence

In urban centres people are so busy just going about their normal business. Busy people move very fast, trying to catch time or buy into it. When a friend meets you, you either say, "hi" and move on, or pause awhile, chat a little and continue.

There are many people who you have seen but passed by. Either you or they may not have cared if the other existed. You only talk with people you know. But there are times when you will come across these uncommon people at the airport departure lounge or wharf or in other places away from your locality.

It was a Monday in July 2019 as I sat waiting at the Buka airport departure lounge. I met this fine wantok Apo. We were both waiting for Air Niugini but going to different destinations. I was waiting to go to Rabaul and he to Port Moresby.

I broke the ice with conversation while waiting for the plane. We knew each other. I said I was going to Rabaul, and he to the nation's capital, Port Moresby. He asked me where I was from. A question I should have asked before we even began talking.

"I am from EHP," I said. "I already knew you were from Goroka (a slang meaning Eastern Highlands Province) by your Tok Pisin."

He said he was part Bougainville and EHP-Korofeigu (Bena Bena) to be exact. "We're not strangers but wantoks," he said. Another country man from Apoland.

We were busy with our conversation and the time slipped away. It was 11:30am, the national flag carrier's Estimated Time of Arrival (ETA), when our conversation was disturbed by a female's voice announcing, "PX 253 to Tokua and then onto Port Moresby is delayed by 90 minutes." As the airport needs more development such as fencing, which is in progress, she didn't even need a PA system to inform the waiting, expectant passengers. Unlike Aropa airport in central Bougainville, Buka needs more development. Without the aid of this very important instrument, she talked so casually.

We ended our conversation and my friend went out. I looked after our luggage. As I had nothing to read, I kept myself busy reading old emails on my mobile.

Around what seemed to be half an hour later he showed up with two Big Rooster lunch packs and two Vita juices. The food he bought was something I occasionally take. I didn't tell him I don't take these food stuffs very often, but his instincts may have spoken to him that day. Fast food is the main culprit of lifestyle disease, so I don't eat it. At least no soft drink, something I don't drink as food.

We sat there in the lounge and had our food. As we unpacked, he whispered, "We have started a chain reaction". From the corner of our eyes, we saw the passengers going out one by one to look for something to eat as it was nearing 12 o'clock. The little that was eaten earlier that morning wasn't enough to keep everyone going for the next one and a half hours.

It wasn't long before our carry-on-luggage was rechecked. This was due to the flight delay. The security guards did a thorough check for this flight and the first flight. But there was a huge chance of smuggling prohibited items here. I recalled the very first words from a church leader when I arrived here a year ago. "Bougainville is different."

When the last passenger passed through the security check, the Fokker 100 from Kieta landed. We parted company as we boarded the plane.

Grandma's K20 Coins

My maternal grandma was such a nice, hospitable person and someone it was good to be around. She had a sense of humour that attracted us kids. When we had time, we enjoyed her company. We would even play with her, but not in front of our parents. Our custom didn't allow that.

On the other hand, grandpa was so reclusive and didn't like noise and misbehaviour. He loved us as any grandparents would do as long as we adhered to his instructions.

As a member of a patrilineal society, I didn't have much time with my mother's people. We got along when we could because of the social boundaries that existed between us, which we weren't allowed to breach.

My eldest sister Judy was raised by our maternal grandparents. Both parties had to come to terms and made it culturally legal for adoption. Since then we have missed her a lot.

Judy observed that grandmother had in her possession K20.00 of kina coins, which would rattle when she walked about. The coins were laced in a woollen knitted rope. When she needed to make a purchase she would remove a kina and replace it with a new one.

One day my sister Judy asked if she could change the coins into notes for convenience sake. She agreed without a protest.

About 10 minutes later, Judy emerged from the house and handed her a K20 note. Grandmother sat there and stared hard at it for a long time without saying a word. She refused to take the note and shouted at Judy. "Where is my money? I gave you 20 kina in coins." She demonstrated with the count of her fingers and toes. "This is how much I gave you. You can't fool me. Don't think that I am an old lady that you can fool around with," she said. "You can do that to others but not me. I am just as intelligent as you."

Judy smiled and tried to explain the situation, but her explanation was like water off a duck's back. Grandmother had turned into an ogre she couldn't stand up to!

Judy consoled herself that she had confronted a person slowly accepting change and who has yet to understand many things. She returned her coin money back without hesitation.

Old people do not understand many things the younger generation accept easily. This is because of the generation gap. They will do and say funny things but we accept them because they are going finish.

The Tool that Became a Weapon

It was a dry season in Bulolo town this time. Not the absence of rain but the absence of *buai* or betelnut. Some call it the 'green gold', an expression used with vanilla in the late 1990s and early 2000. A period when the vanilla price was very high, and it fetched above the world price.

My in-law, seeing the demand for this tropical nut, shipped in about three 60 kilogram bags from the island of Siassi to Lae. His son brought them to Bulolo by Public Motor Vehicle (PMV).

As soon as the prized nuts arrived at their destination, customers came in numbers to buy them. The sales went very well. Some were sold at the town's main market. Most times the house sales continued right into the night.

His family made some good money. They decided to ship in the next lot, this time quadruple the number.

Within two days the supply was down to a quarter of a bag. It was decided that the next day his son will go down to Lae for the new supply.

That afternoon the sales went as usual and continued on into the night. At ten o'clock they packed away the remainder and went to bed while the old man sat in his *hauswin* by the fire. An hour later he saw a dim flashlight approaching. He laid back on his mat suspecting the boys on their usual rounds to the neighbour's house for a smoke.

He was woken up by the sharp tip of a knife pressed against his chest. "Give us the money or else I will drive this knife into your heart." He could feel the knife piercing his frail old skin.

The frightened old man called his wife. "Atak, open the door, customers are here for buai." The wife opened the door hoping to see customers but instead saw her husband.

"Where are the customers?" she said rather angrily as she was also woken up late in the night. Atak didn't complete her sentence before she felt the sharp point of a knife penetrating her neck from someone at the side of the door.

"Give us the money or we will take your lives." She got the shock of her life as her water broke lose.

As soon as the money was handed to them, the robbers fled the scene to the safety of the nearby bushes. The couple raised the alarm but it was too late. The family lost K2,600.00 to the robbers that night.

When everyone came, they could see the knife which was used as a weapon still lying there where the robbers had left it. When the son who slept in the boy's house identified the bush knife, he got really cross with the couple. One of the robbers later became his in-law and got married to his daughter.

Don't leave your tools outside when you go to sleep, they can be used as weapon against you.

My Papa and Mama's Bank

It was the coffee season. Coffee fetched a high price because of the world commodity price that year. It picked up very well and remained so for two months. Small block coffee owners made a lot of money. "Be in the race or be left behind," was a common slogan on the lips of every adult and able citizen of this far flung Okapa district.

Papa had a sizeable coffee garden. He had planted it when he returned home from Rabaul after his coconut plantation labour contract expired in 1971. Seeing that he had married and would soon have kids, he decided to plant more coffee gardens.

By the time I was born 3 years later in 1974, he had three gardens. But there was one problem that stood in his way and that was the management and upkeep of the gardens. Because it was labour intensive, he needed extra helping hands to help look after the gardens as well as harvesting.

To solve this problem, he married my second mama when I was 12 years old. Yet at a heavy cost, much to the added expense of his extended family members, but a worthwhile reciprocal help. To the many extended family members his second wife's bride price was a waste and a financial burden which should have been avoided. On the other hand, my father was adamant that it was worth it.

The extended family was proven wrong when his second wife brought in much needed extra labour for the family. The family coffee gardens benefited as well with a high output in cash. Father thought he was financially secure and that he could do anything since his young family was small and manageable. That is when he learned the skill of money management.

When there was a funeral or bride price payment, he could financially help as he had the access to money. As a kid I watched him and mama opening their locked red 30cm x 30cm x 30cm money box. He would bring out the set of keys, hidden from us kids, hung somewhere in a secluded part of the house only known to him and mama.

Looking inside, I was like, "Wow! There was lots and lots of money," K20 notes, K10 notes, K5 notes and K2 notes, with the coins in a mail bag. They were all paper notes with the exception of K50 and K100 notes, which weren't available in those days. The notes were fastened with rubber bands with small notes slid in. They were written in pen. What I didn't know was that he had money belonging to my grandparents as well as his sisters in the box, because he was the only boy in a tribe of girls. Also placed beside the parcels of money were small booklets containing money. All the money kept there was for different purposes.

When I went to school, he took out only my school fee money, he never touched the others. When his cousin brothers got married, he would contribute from the money that he set aside, never dipping his hands into the others.

My father was only a standard one student, but he was already a banker where he kept different accounts in this mini-bank. He knew how much he withdrew and how much was left. I now admire his simple book-keeping skills which I never appreciated as a child.

One day mama said, "We need a new book to do the banking. We are running out of pages." Why is she talking to me regarding money, I am just a child unable to advise her?

"Okay," I said. My mother listened attentively as if my words seemed to have solved her problem. "Ask father to buy one from town."

Because father and I went to town last week and saw many books on display, I was sure bookshops and second-hand dealers in Goroka were selling them at an affordable price. But she wanted a free book from the school library. Mama said they couldn't afford to waste money on books which have no real value even if they decide on one.

She checked up on me and pestered every day to get a book from the school library. I was so scared I told my mother I wouldn't do that for fear of being flogged publicly. She said, "But we badly need the book, there's nobody beside you can help." There was nothing I could do but make an attempt at it.

I finally took the library book after several attempts. It was lunch and the library was opened for students to pass the time reading. Not many students realised the importance of reading and utilised it. Most went into the library just to see pictures, with only a few genuine readers.

I easily picked one on cars, beginning with the invention of the steam engine, to the early cars, to the recent past, current and the look of future cars which could be powered by solar power, something that has become a reality today in developed countries.

On this particular day there was no librarian to check at the door and I took the chance to walk out with it. It was through this loophole that many books were smuggled out. This ill-supplied library was a simple building with books properly stacked on shelves in the middle and reading space all around.

I looked from side to side to make sure nobody was watching as I feared being punished the same way as other law breakers. To make matters worse, my father was a member of the School Board of Management and I dreaded their reaction to it if I was caught. I saw them caning my class mate the other day. He was an older student in his twenties. I couldn't forget the look on his face. His face was red, fearful and perspiring.

Anyway I made a dash for the fence and jumped over it as though I was being chased, finally making it home through the thick overgrowth.

My mother couldn't thank me enough for undertaking this risky task. She finally had her prized possession. That was my first and last time. I never stole from the school again as I feared being flogged, as I had witnessed often with my school mates.

The Invisible Barrier

We were within inches of each other. I was there to make sure everything was fine before they could go. My heart bled for my daughter, the only one in a tribe of boys, who was going to Port Moresby with her mum for her uncle's graduation at PNGEI on the 5th of December 2019. Her mum was at the check-in counter to sort out their luggage. I was with the baby at the back looking on.

In the dying moments before the plane arrived, I cuddled my daughter close to my heart and wished she wasn't going. While I was lost in my own world, unconscious of the surroundings, my wife interrupted me, *"Tarangu pikinini ya ino save olsem em bai flai long balus."* [Poor child she doesn't know she is flying on a plane.] This brought tears to me but I fought them back. Men don't weep in public.

As I was advising my wife about the dangers of the city, I had a tap on my shoulder. I turned to see the National Airports Co-operation (NAC) guard. "Excuse me Sir, could you go sit outside?" I protested. I was there to leave my wife and kid to go. But he told me it was NAC policy that only those who are boarding the plane will be allowed in the departure lounge.

With a heavy heart I left the departure lounge. Two hours earlier, I was sitting with the child in my arms next to my wife. We came into Buka town from Devare Adventist High School the previous day because they were to check in at 9:00 am (BST) Bougainville Standard Time, which in PNG mainland time would be 8:30 am.

I took a last look at them from outside the fence as they entered the plane and it wheeled off. People were waving, others were crying. In the deafening sound of the take-off I turned and walked to the bus stop.

While heading to town, I thought of the many invisible lines that cut across land boundaries separating families and ethnic groups.

I thought of the new nation of Bougainville which is in the making. With intermarriage we have relatives on both sides. Two of my brothers are married to Bougainvillean women. I thought of how their wives would feel when they are separated from their families.

Then I thought of the other half of the island of New Guinea, West Papua and their cries for freedom. They may be allowed as traditional border crossers to see each other. Due to the current turn of political events, families are stranded on both sides and as Melanesians we feel for them. When would they be free from foreign rule and be independent?

Also the North and South Koreans with families and relatives on both sides. Even though both governments allowed them once to meet with their families after so many years between them, they have a deep hunger and yearning that one day they will be united as one people.

When Uncles Were a Step Ahead of Grandmother

Like all young people, my uncles were so cheeky and cunning. They would do anything that made them feel proud. They wanted people to say something good and positive about them. They did many things that would steal the show.

The third born was the cheekiest of them all. The others learnt from him. He had a real sense of humour. He was so charming and invented many new tricks to avoid being punished. Grandma had the habit of checking up on every nitty-gritty thing both inside and outside the house. She was good in taking a mental stock-take of the things the family owned. Because of this unique attitude of grandma, they would call her a parrot whose eyes can take a quick stock-take of what is there and what is not, or has gone missing.

They attended school at the community school in the village. Because of the nearness of the school to the village, they didn't carry their lunch with them. This was not according to the rules. All school children were asked to bring their own lunch. Those who couldn't bring theirs resorted to stealing. This was controlled by harsh punishment which the parents supported. But this didn't deter many boys from stealing. They found their own ways around it.

My uncles invented this stealing technique which even the parrot-eyed grandmother couldn't detect.

It was a fine Sunday afternoon and Grandmother was busy knitting her new bilum. The tree bark was so rigid she had to use her frail old hands skilfully and carefully to beat and soften it. Her aging eyes deterred her from completing the task in minimum time. As she worked, she thought of the time when she was young with good eyes completing this same task quickly and on time. But she made progress, slow work, but a fine job. The old man was sitting opposite her, busy making a bow. As he chiselled away at the split palm, he sang his old favourite song, entertaining the old woman who hummed to the song, bringing out a rich traditional melody.

Uncle Jacob returned from the river with his laundry, wrung it out and dried it on the clothesline. He heard the couple singing and thought, "What a beautiful day for hunting?" Let the old happy pair sing and reminisce about their good old days. He walked into the kunai thatched house to pick up his bilum (string bag), bow and arrows. While making his way out he spotted some coins in his mother's bilum. He peeped to make sure his mother or his sisters were not coming his way. If they were, he would be in serious trouble with grandmum. He was thankful that his sisters had gone to the garden at sunrise and hadn't returned yet. Uncle quickly dropped a 50t coin into his mouth and swallowed it, along with the many coins that his mother left unattended in her busyness.

In the afternoon Jacob came home only to be greeted with complaints from grandmother, accusing him and his brothers of stealing. He complained to his mother for singling him out when things went missing. "Why am I being blamed all the time when things go missing? Am I the only one around?" Jacob would mumble to himself. Grandmum did a thorough check on him, and to her disappointment found nothing. From his reactions she knew it was Jacob but could not prove her suspicions without tangible evidence.

The next day was Monday, Jacob and his brothers went to school. When nature's call came he visited the bush instead of the toilet. Why the bush instead of the toilet? Well the reason was to check up on the deposited money. He spread the excrement apart and checked for the coin. When he had found the coin, he washed it and bought his lunch with it.

When this misdeed was successful, he stole more coins from his family and escaped without being caught. Slowly his brother followed in his shoes. Not long after, all of them got involved in this act of stealing. Whenever they had the chance to come across a coin they would swallow it. Their mother didn't know their technique of stealing until they became men.

Note: Don't try this as it may cause some health problems.

I am Missing Something

They met while at the Balob Teachers' College. Angku (central Buang for the title of 1st born boy) was doing his 2nd year, while Muing (central Buang for the title of 1st born girl) was doing her final year. She eyed this young energetic Morobean bloke from the Patrol Post but was too shy to approach him. She was Morobean as well but from the valley.

Before long Angku quickly picked up her body language. He decided that one day he would approach her and prove his suspicion about her as a man.

It was Thursday evening, special mealtime. Thursdays every week the students were treated to special meals. Apart from the normal meal of rice and tinned fish with cabbage, they would be supplemented with lamb, beef or chicken stew. When the students complained of eating Besta tinned fish and cabbage, the mess supervisor would smile and say, "Now you're tired of eating the same menu but when you work you will not be able to afford to buy lamb flaps, beef or chicken. Tinned fish and rice will be your main stable food." The students ate without any thought of the supervisor's words which proved to be true in the work field.

When the evening mess bell rang, Angku ran into the shower and had his wash. He rushed to his cubicle and selected the best attire for this meeting. He joined the already lengthening queue. From time to time, he would chirp over the shoulders of his friends to the girls' line. He could see the familiar dress among the girls. He no doubt thought she was there.

Angku soon found himself at the mess door. From this distance he had the advantage of seeing the love of his life. When he turned to see the girl in that familiar dress, he was disappointed to see not Muing but her girlfriend. She must have borrowed the dress from her. Well, no need to ask if she had seen her for fear of embarrassment given that serious look of dislike. What if she tells him off in front of everyone? Questions went up in his mind. Where could she be? Has she lied to him? No, this couldn't be possible. He trusted his instincts. The many signs in the body language he saw in Muing was just enough. She must have gone in earlier.

He finally entered the door. There were already many students inside. The mess was a beehive. Students were talking, chatting away while some were walking out with their empty plates and others with their servings looking for a space to sit.

After being served he looked for a seat to sit at. All tables were filled with students but there was one which looked more inviting. It was the girls' corner. Someone was sitting there and stared at him as she ate her food, and stared again. That was the signal for him. He walked over to the table and sat next to her. What a feeling of joy and excitement. He felt content.

"Good afternoon." The girl spoke first. "Were you the one who came in the green bus yesterday from town?"

"Yes," nodding his head in almost a whisper. "And where are you from?" Before Angku had time to reply, she said "I guess you're from Morobe Patrol Post."

Wow! She must have been doing her research prior to meeting me, he thought.

When he finally had the courage to speak, the chapel bell rang and they had to part. They promised to meet in the library after worship.

What a feeling it was for the boy. He was on top of the world. That short conversation set the footings for their later frequent get together and talks.

They met in the library briefly and separated because Muing had a science oral seminar presentation in the hall, while Angku had to complete an assignment next day.

From then on they met regularly but had to take extra precaution for if the college securities found them in dark corners it would be trouble. They could be expelled from studies. A fraction of the students has been referred to the Governing Council for possible expulsion.

Just last week they saw Awong of Kabwum and his girlfriend Avade of Lufa walking out of the campus with tears in their eyes. What would they say to their parents who have sacrificed so much to pay their tuition fees?

Sunday afternoon October the 18th, is a day she will never forget. The day the boy made the proposal to her. "Will you marry me?" he asked.

The Saturday night movie scene came vividly to her. The prince asking the country girl to marry him. "Give me time to think and come back to you later," she replied.

That same afternoon she wrote to him saying that the proposal was accepted. This was the best decision she had made. She knew he was the man she would live with for the rest of her life. He even promised all the goodies. "I will look after you. I am the man you wouldn't want to lose."

Seeing her friends and classmates pairing off every year after graduation, made her to think "Why not me?"

Because the girl was graduating at the end of the year, they proposed to have their wedding a week after. The girl's parents proposed a church wedding which the boy reluctantly accepted.

Two months before the graduation they got engaged in front of their relatives. After the event the girl's parents noticed something. *"Mama yu lukim meri ya tu? Mi lukim olsem pikinini meri ya gat hevi ya,"* whispered the father.

"Mi tu lukim na laik askim long en yu tok," said the wife. The mother called her daughter aside and asked if the signs she saw in her was true. At this opportune time she also announced to her mother that she was two months pregnant.

When the news of the engagement reached the boy's parents, they objected to it. But the brothers thought it was the best decision to marry another teacher who could be of monetary benefit to the family.

The boy bought her the graduation clothes and presented them to her. "How kind of you, my man," she said. "I am yours, my body, my soul and whole." She saw herself lucky to be engaged to him and would soon be married to someone as caring as he. Two days ago, he had pestered his elder sister who works at Eriku's Raumai 18, an Asian shop, to give him some money for the dress.

During the graduation both the boy's and girl's relatives turned up to witness. It was a joyous moment for the girl's relatives as the first in her family to finally graduate. Angku was the happiest man among them. He could dream and usher in the expected event soon after.

After the celebrations were over, the girl's father opted for his daughter's wedding to be held the following Sunday after the worship service. Both of them were devout Lutherans, a Christian denomination.

That week was a busy week for both the couple and their parents. Everything was ready before Saturday, the wedding dress and suit as well as food. The boy's parents made a boat convoy from across the Patrol post to Lae where the wedding was to take place. The girl's relatives came in a truck load from up the Markham valley with lots of bananas (*marafris*) and other garden food stuff.

On Saturday night, friends and all other relatives gathered at the girl's parent's house. The family residence at Kamkumung was packed. Angku's family also gathered at his uncle's residence at 3mile along the Highlands Highway.

Both families had their Sunday service at Our Saviour's Lutheran church at Eriku next to the Bumbu Police Barracks, as this was the wedding venue. The church family was ready too. Balloons, palms leaves and other decorations littered the church compound. The church itself was dressed up in Morobe colours; green, blue, orange and white balloons. From the church door to the pulpit was red carpet.

The church service coincided with the wedding. Family and friends of the bride and groom were seated upfront on both sides of the pew.

After a short service the wedding program kicked off and lasted for three hours. When the marriage formalities were done the family headed to Kamkumung where traditional rites and obligations were done and tied.

Angku took his wife Muing to Morobe Patrol Post and spent the Christmas vacation there. But they had to return to Lae before the New Year eve despite Angku's parents' insistence to stay until the second week of January. They had to check for teacher postings at the education office which would be posted in the first week of January so that teachers can have ample time to prepare for their new postings.

On Monday morning they took a bus from 3 mile to top town. The education office was already packed with both the serving teachers as well as new graduates. The teaching postings were displayed in alphabetical order by districts beginning with the Bulolo district.

Muing took up a teaching position at Wagau primary school in the Buang LLG of Bulolo district Morobe province. She was excited as it was her first teaching post. Angku objected but had no choice than to except it.

Angku went back to the college to complete his studies while Muing willingly took up the teaching post at Wagau. They agreed to meet on the first term break. That is when she would already be put on pay.

Three weeks before the first term break, Angku made a surprise visit to Wagau primary school. The wife took a surprise look at her husband. "Darling I was expecting you in three weeks' time," she said.

He didn't say anything but the look on his face told her something was not right. "Can't you have respect? I have just arrived. Give me time to settle down and I will explain my reason for coming."

He found it hard to force these words out, clenched his fist and punched her, sending her backward down on the floor with a big BANG! Before Muing knew what was happening he sent the kitchen utensils flying rattling through the window onto the lawn outside.

The teacher next door came running to the scene. "What's wrong?" There was no response to this question. Angku's sister emerged from the room and explained to the teacher and those who gathered. Not long after, the head teacher, Mr. Albert Tato, appeared. When Angku knew that the head teacher was around, he went into the kitchen and sat down quietly while Muing went into her bedroom, locked the door after her and sobbed.

Mr. Tato had to go back to his house as none of the couple was willing to respond to his queries.

In the room Muing felt her world was falling apart. She reminisced on their first meetings and the honey sweet talks she received from him. She sobbed and fought hard to dismiss the thought of breaking up. But she was married in church, what would her friends think of her? And the church family?

Her husband's real self was finally exposed. He was a bad-tempered person who she will now come to live with for the rest of her life.

The Runaway Priest

He was born in 1945, three years before the WW2 ended in 1948. Not attended by a midwife nor born on a comfortable hospital bed. He was brought into this world in a cave during the war in the Siwai district of South Bougainville.

He cried a lot as an infant, so that his father, being an Australian Scout, proposed to his wife one day to kill the baby to avoid being pried upon by the cunning merciless Japanese who had a permanent base not far away in Guadalcanal in the Solomon Islands. "They will wipe us out if they hear the slightest noise of the infant's cry," said the father fearfully.

"Are you serious?" his wife asked.

"I am only proposing it and you think about it," he responded.

"I would rather think you never said that," said the wife sternly. "You didn't feel the birth pangs I felt. Leave it to me, I will handle it my way." This gagged his mouth and he retreated to his duty in silence.

When he was three years old the war finally ended in favour of the US and her allies, Australia and Great Britain. Since then he was known as mummy's boy. He did all his mother asked him to do.

Joe attended school with the concern of his mother, while the boys of his age roamed free in the village. They had nothing to do with the white man's institution. School to the natives was something new and they didn't know what it held for their future. The parents didn't bother sending their kids to school. Even Joe's father didn't care if any of his kids went to school. But it was through his mother's persistence that he continued his primary school.

Many of his classmates left school without completing the six years of their primary education. They saw that they were in the white man's institution wasting their time instead of engaging in worthwhile activities like hunting, fishing or gardening.

His parish priest asked him one day. "What would you like to become after completing your education?"

"Umm, I'd like to be like you," he replied shyly. Joe admired working as a priest and a policeman but since a priest was asking, he had to tell the priest this.

When he finished his grade 6 (standard six in those days) he was ushered into the Catholic boys camp at Sohano island to be trained as a priest. After three months of induction on the island they would be sent to Channel minor seminary in Rabaul for their training proper.

It was arranged that the next day, a boat would take them from Buka to Rabaul. The boys were so excited, but time was running out for Joe. Word was going around that a police recruiting officer was on Buka Island. That night he sneaked out from the camp, borrowed a canoe from a local, and paddled to Kamarau, Buka. He went straight to the recruiting officer's house and knocked.

"Come in, please!" said a voice from inside. A tall white officer answered the door. "Yes, young man, what can I do for you?"

"I heard," said Joe, "that there's a police recruiting officer here."

Before giving Joe time to complete his words, the officer said. "Stand there," pointing towards the door.

There were numbers written with marker in an ascending order. "So, you want to become a policeman ah?" he continued.

"Yes, sir!" Joe replied confidently.

"A police vehicle will pick you up from the wharf tomorrow," concluded the officer.

Joe left Kamarau jubilantly and slipped back into the camp quietly just as he went out without the priest knowing it.

The next day as expected a boat from Rabaul came into the wharf. After all formalities were done by the priest they got on the boat.

As they were approaching Matupit and the boat was manoeuvring into the wharf, Joe excitedly told his friends from Siwai and other areas in the south that a police vehicle will be waiting for them at the wharf. As soon as they came out of the boat, sure enough there was a police vehicle waiting there.

A policeman came out of the vehicle and said, *"Yupela ol boi Buka laka? Mipela painim wanpela boi bilong Buka ya, nem bilong en em Joe"* [Are you boys from Buka? We are looking for Joe a boy from Buka who may be among your company].

Everyone turned to Joe. "Yes sir. I'm here," shouted Joe. The Bougainvillean boys didn't believe what was transpiring, how can just a simple boy like Joe be known by the police and given this special treatment? They stood there bewildered.

What would the priest say if he ever finds out, murmured the boys among themselves. Without giving enough time to answer their questions, Joe got his few belongings and hopped on the vehicle. But the policeman signalled him into the front, and they drove off. That was the last time they ever saw Joe again.

After completing his police training at Tomaringa Police Barracks he worked with the newly established Royal Papua New Guinea Constabulary as a cadet back in his home province of North Solomons. Later he climbed the promotion ladder to becoming a PPC, taught briefly at the Bomana Police College and later resigned. He worked with SP Brewery and Oregen Minerals as security manager, travelled the world and now at 75years of age he is back in his home province.

Armed with his grade six certificate he climbed to the top of the promotional ladder. What was his secret? His secret is his sheer determination to succeed and compete in the competitive world. He says, "Never say I can't when you can." Just believe in yourself that you can. Be obedient to your parents and you will see great results.

Ephesians 6:1-3. (NIV) *"Children, obey your parents in the Lord, for this is right. Honour your father and mother"- which is the first commandment with a promise - that it may go well with you and that you may enjoy long life on the earth."*

The Slain Opportunity

Simon comes from Paipindi village near Ivingoi area in the South Fore constituency of the Okapa district, Eastern Highlands province. He grew up just like any other kid and went to school at the nearby Ivingoi Community School. Having dropped out of school in Grade 6, he decided to go to Port Moresby with his friends, in search of better life opportunities. He stayed with his friends at Gordons. As a Grade 6 leaver, he couldn't find a job as his grade six certificate had little or no value. But Grade 10s could at least find jobs.

One day as usual he decided to stroll around town. He hopped on a PMV bus to Boroko but got tired of going from shop to shop doing window shopping. So Simon decided to hurry back to the bus stop to catch the bus to Gordons.

As he walked past one of the fenced houses, he heard a whistle as if someone was signalling him. When he looked inside the fenced wall, there was an old white lady in her 60s. She motioned him to the gate. *"Mi painim wanpela boi long wok long haus bilong mi. Yu inap wok?"* asked the old lady. Though Simon was surprised with the fluency of her Tok Pisin, without a second thought he accepted the offer.

He started work the next day as a house helper. Simon was such a faithful and trustworthy worker that he was called in to share the accommodation with the couple a few weeks later.

Before long he started to come to understand the white man's world. Budgeting and managing money, even the little, were instilled in this young man. What a privilege as it would help him later in life.

But all good things must come to an end. Simon worked for about two years. The couple's work contract expired and they had to return back to Australia at the end of that year. They got Simon's home address[4] and left, promising him that they would contact him as soon as they settled in Australia.

After what seemed to be a year and a half, Simon received his much-anticipated letter from the couple. Simon's relative saw a letter bearing his name in the school's canteen and informed him when he returned from the usual Monday market at Ivingoi.

Early the next day he went up to the school and got his letter. He opened it and read a short five sentence message. Simon ran his eyes down the letter and a highlighted and capitalized sentence caught his eyes which read,

"YOUR PLANE TICKET IS READY FOR PICK UP AT GOROKA POST OFFICE."

Is this for real or am I dreaming?

He closed the letter and read it again. He digested every content of the message. "Ohh! Ohh! I am going." "Ohh! Ohh! I am going."

Three days later, he left his village for Goroka. After two hours of tiring trip he finally arrived at Goroka. He was dropped off at West Goroka bus stop. He paid his PMV fare and headed to the town Post Office.

As he approached the Post Office, his heart began to beat faster. What am I going to say, I am just a simple village boy? He assured himself that he would try to be brave. Simon joined the queue at the post office. When his turn came, he presented the letter at the counter. "Is this your letter?" asked the lady behind the counter.

"Yes, ma-am, it's mine," mumbled Simon.

"Then present your ID, she continued, as well so we can verify it's yours and not someone else." Simon protested he didn't have the ID; he was just a village boy.

"Okay, do you know anyone working in Goroka who can identify you?" Simon nodded and walked out. "And come back any time today so I can help you," the lady called after him.

With a worried look and head bowed Simon walked not knowing where to find someone to assist him. He heard people conversing

---

4. Simon as a village boy didn't have an address of his own. This was his old primary school's address.

in his local Fore dialect. He turned to see who they were and to his surprise saw one of the former Okapa MPs with his cohorts. This was Simon's golden opportunity or let it slip by. He tried to approach the MP. "Hello member, I huh I huh," Simon tried to force words out. "Yes son, how can I help you?"

Simon explained everything and together they walked back to the post office. This time they didn't wait at the counter to be served but went straight to the lady. "Yes sir, how may I help you?"

"I am here to identify this young man to get his tickets," said the MP. The lady gave Simon a white envelope containing his ticket without further question.

Outside Simon thanked the MP and parted. He walked down to the Peace Park, sat down under one of the trees, pulled out his prized envelope, slid it open and emptied the contents. There was some money for the plane ticket to Port Moresby but no money for his expenses in the city. When he checked his waist bag there were two twenty kina notes and a fifty kina. This was just enough for the one week he would be in POM.

It was a usual cold morning when he left for Moresby the next day. From the window he took his last look at Goroka, which represented his home. He wondered if he would ever fly back into Goroka someday. Minutes later the plane wheeled into the Jackson's International Airport, Port Moresby.

The following week was a busy week for him as he got his documents in order. The passport especially was time consuming but before week's end he got it. The same day he presented the letter (this was the letter he received from the couple) at the Australian embassy and got his visa as well. Now all set for departure. He thanked his friends for helping him get the documents on time.

Simon couldn't forget this day, Tuesday. He stood in the departure lounge at Jackson's airport. He asked for the international flights check in counter and got his ticket checked.

Some twenty minutes later, the boarding call came. He got his bag and joined the passengers towards the departing gate. Most of them were expatriates. His heart beat fast as he boarded Air Niugini, the national flag carrier.

During the flight he didn't eat anything provided by the cabin crew. This was not because he wasn't hungry but because of the fear that he may not make it to his final destination because he was to make a transit at one of the airports. In addition to his fear was his inability to speak good English. The flight took him to Sydney. He didn't believe he was in Sydney. He thought he was dreaming.

He got off at Sydney and waited for his next boarding call. Because he couldn't make sense of what was being aired over the Public Address System nor could he read the writing on the screen, he asked the Papua New Guinean air hostess for help. He showed her his ticket and was referred to a section where people were already queuing up. He stood in the line until evening. Every one of the people in his queue were all gone accept him. Simon sat there not knowing what to do. Someone tapped him on the shoulder and turned to face a white security guard. "Young man, are you alright?" Simon couldn't control his emotions and he wept openly relieving his anxiety. And in broken English explained what happened. What Simon didn't know was that he was at the wrong departure lounge. He blamed the female Air Niugini cabin crew for this mishap. How can a wantok fool her own country man?

The guard got his ticket, scribbled something on a piece of paper and send him to the correct departure lounge. This guard was so helpful that he contacted the couple and told them what happened to their visitor. Because of this experience the couple and the guard made all things possible. This time he didn't have to worry.

Finally, he got on the plane for his last leg of the journey. When he got off at the final airport,[5] lo and behold! Waiting right there in front of everybody was his old man. They embraced each other and tears of joy flowed freely for they had finally found each other.

The couple drove him to their country home. And he stayed there for three months. During his stay there he got to see a few places in that state. Because he couldn't communicate well in English, he couldn't move around by himself but spent time caring for the home.

---

5. When I interviewed Simon about this airport, he said he can't remember the name. What we all need to understand is that because of his limited education he can't help us with the name.

Simon didn't stay long. He was sick and had to be sent back to PNG. The couple did all they could by taking him to the hospital, but this didn't help much. Simon blamed his sickness on witchcraft (poisin). He was worried that he wouldn't survive without him taking *skin diwai*.[6] He regrets having made that foolish decision.

---

6. A name for traditional doctor's healing herbs. Poisin or witchcraft is believed to be cured only by herbs.

A Mother's Quest for Education

The ten year old Bougainville crisis which started in 1989 was so devastating, taking away more than 20,000 lives, causing scars only slowly healing. Many hundreds were displaced in the neighbouring Solomon Islands and Papua New Guinea. Seared relationships remained among the Bougainvilleans themselves, the rest of the Papua New Guineans and above all the PNG Defence Force soldiers who took part in the operations.

A Kongara lass of Central Bougainville was doing her 1st year studying Surveying and Land Management at Unitech (University of Technology) when the Crisis began in 1989, ending her promising career. She therefore withdrew from Studies and returned to Bougainville. What she didn't know was that this was the last flight in and out of Bougainville as the Crisis heightened.

The first sign that greeted her was Aropa airport, burnt to ashes. Months before she left, it had a world standard airport facility, the best in the whole of Papua New Guinea including the Pacific. Outside of Australia and New Zealand it was indeed a "pearl in the Pacific". The Australian government made Bougainville the most developed and westernized area in the whole of the Pacific. This was made possible by the Australian mining giant Rio Tinto which was owned by the Panguna Mining or Bougainville Copper Limited. These were now just dreams of yesteryears.

Peninah came from a well to do family. The crisis took away all that the family had built over the years. Business, with all its assets such as trucks including the family home, were either burned or personalized by the rebels.

The Crisis changed everything. Peace and normalcy were evaporating very fast in this once tropical paradise. Peninah and all the females of marriageable age were very susceptible to rape and physical abuse from both the BRA and the PNG Defence Force soldiers.

To avoid all sorts of abuse the best thing she thought was to get married, but also to have someone who could help her complete her studies after the Crisis. She got married to a primary school teacher.

In 1993 at the height of the crisis the husband-and-wife team left Bougainville to study at Pacific Adventist University (PAU) near Port Moresby, Papua New Guinea.

A letter was sent from the Bougainville Mission of the Seventh Day Adventist Church at Rumba. The bearer didn't explain further. All he said was, *"Leta bilong yu ol lain long Rumba givim."* With these few words he left. He has to do this for his own safety because you can be killed on suspicion of being a traitor or betrayal. This was a risky undertaking. Eyes were watching him from both the Bougainville Revolutionary Army (BRA) and the Bougainville Resistance forces. Peninah quickly tucked away the letter in her already worn-out skirt to be read later with her husband when nobody was around.

When opportunity struck the next day, she slipped her shaking hand into her skirt pocket and pulled out the letter. It was wet from sweat at the places where fingers touched it. One could literally see this. They peeped over their shoulders every now and then to make sure nobody was prying around or someone could run at them yelling and shouting. The thump, thump in her chest could even be heard by a bystander. She quickly whispered a prayer for God's protection and guidance as she silently read the letter and passed it to her husband who was sitting next to her. He was already soaked to the skin from perspiration.

This was the acceptance letter from PAU to study Bachelor of Arts degree in Secondary school teaching. Their joy swelled up, but they could not push it out. Maybe reserve it until later when normalcy returns. She had applied the previous year but forgot all about it. Nobody was allowed to travel out of the island except the mission President Pr Jeffrey Paul. It was the president who did all the arrangements for her study. Praise God for him. They later found out that because of the blockade, the acceptance letter came through the Solomon Islands mission in Honiara.

Peninah was determined to go so as was her husband, Enoch. The path before them was tough with the blockade already in place. No civilians were allowed to move around. They prayed everyday so that things would work out in their favour. They wrote to the BRA commander Mr. Ismael Toroama who controlled that area. They prayed and waited for the response. Their request was granted, that the commander himself would take them to Sirovai where they were to catch the only boat, with a 40 horsepower engine.

The next day, Sunday, the commander himself dropped them at their place of departure. They left at 5 o'clock in the evening and passed through the enemy territory. It was a starless night. At some points along the way, the boat skipper had to put off the engine and let it adrift for fear of the Forces on the island.

It took them six hours and by midnight they found themselves on Taro Island in the Solomon Islands territory. This is the island closest to Bougainville. They stayed there for a week. The islanders looked after them well on humanitarian grounds as refugees. Because of the closeness of the island, most of the islanders were related to the Bougainvilleans, especially South Bougainville.

They praised God for His protection and whispered a prayer of thanks. It was God's intervention as they found out that they were the last group to cross over the PNG Solomon Islands border. A total blockade was imposed after that keeping families separated for the next 10-15 years.

On Sabbath (Saturday) morning the following week, they left on a third level airline for Honiara. After making 5 stops in different places, they arrived at their final destination at 4pm.

Another task lay ahead of them. They did not have a valid travel document and to make matters worse, they were new to Honiara, the Solomon Islands' capital.

After many silent prayers, they decided to go to the airport. What a coincidence that was, as there they bumped into a relative of Enoch, late Mr. Piuki Tasa. Enoch asked if he was related to his clansmen in Kieta and he said he was. What a joy for the couple, another answered prayer. They felt like jumping up and down for joy but assured themselves that they were in a foreign land. Mr. Tasa was there to send his son to Australia for studies. He was the Education Director for the Solomon Island Mission headquarter in Honiara.

After putting his son on the plane, he took them to the mission compound. The church family at the mission compound were anxiously waiting for them. How did they know they were coming? Praise God for Pr Jeffrey Paul, Bougainville Mission president, who did everything he could for the couple. Oh what a relief for them.

Seeing their plight, the Education Director brought their case to the mission Secretary and President, then to the Executive Committee. They stayed in Honiara for about four days while the mission did all necessary arrangements. Before the week was over, the couple were presented with their airline ticket from Honiara to Port Moresby.

They left Honiara happy that the dream was about to be achieved but fearful of retaliation from Papua New Guineans who have lost their relatives in the civil war. It was now into March and classes at PAU had begun 4 weeks ago and registration had ceased.

Late comers were asked to withdraw and come back next year. But for Peninah special consideration was given seeing the situation she was in so that she could still study even though she was late.

Enoch worked as a security guard at the campus to support his wife while she studied. After 4 years of study, she worked and supported her husband so he could also do his degree in secondary teaching.

When the husband completed his studies, they taught at different Adventist High Schools in mainland Papua New Guinea. Not long after an overseas sponsor was looking for a woman from Bougainville to study a Masters in Educational Counselling and Peninah was selected.

The couple with their two young kids, a boy and a girl left for New Zealand for studies. The husband took up studies in management while the wife pursued counselling. After 3 years of study, they were asked to return to Bougainville to help rebuild the crisis torn Island.

Upon their return home they were tasked to start the newly proposed Seventh Day Adventist high school on the Island. This brought them to Inus Point between the north and central districts of Bougainville where they started what is now called Devare Adventist High School.

They have now retired from teaching and reside beside the school today. Many students who have passed out from this school would remember Mr. and Mrs. David.

The Three Months Old Message

After a week of searching by her in-laws, they finally found her. She was comfortable with her new life partner. Not far away was her former village. She had come with her two teenage sons: Willie and Samson from just across the valley.

Sandy had lived there for the past 18 years and the decision to marry again although painful was worth it. She knew this was the best option. Firstly, for the good of her sons who needed a father to raise them up, especially for their education. Besides, at 33 she was still young and attractive. What would stop her from marriage and living her life again? She wouldn't remain a widow wasting her productive life! Yes, Sandy considered the consequences that tantalized her thoughts the moment she left the village. She would be ridiculed for disrespecting her dead husband by not marrying one of her brother-in-laws, which would have resulted in retaining the boys in their father's clan. That would have made her dead husband and deceased father in-law smile.

In fact, that arrangement was a customary obligation pledged at the marriage between her family and her late husband's family. The repercussions if broken were something she wouldn't want to think of. Let it remain buried in her yearning heart, kept from her devastated sons. Nothing could stop the spewing, irritating thoughts. Like the wind they kept coming back. Her in-laws had spent so much in cash and kind for her bride price. Running away with their sons was illegal, incurring hefty fines and court injunctions she would single-handedly shoulder.

Already three months and she had forgotten the haunting thoughts. Sandy and her sons were in the process of adjusting to their new way of life suited to their environment. At first the boys were dumb founded at their mother's indecisiveness. They supposed this didn't happen at all.

Willie and Samson already missed their fathers, mothers and cousins. But first and foremost, their inheritance - the land. They will now start from scratch. Their foster father was contemplating dividing up land between them and his other sons. But the question was, would their half-brothers allow that?

The three-month-old message soon reached Sandy. The new husband was far ahead with his garden implements. Her sons were well behind her. That was aptly a good time to sing the new release as she contemplated the task ahead.

"The hill that I see knows where she is.

My sons and their mother are there.

The place is mosquito infested.

Many heroes have fallen, and

the vast land has eaten its inhabitants.

Poisonous vipers roam free.

My bride, even though my body is earthen,

You're still my wife.

I didn't chase you away.

You're still my wife.

Come home, come back.

I am waiting for you."

Her eyes watered - she couldn't complete singing the song. She lifted her eyes to the land where she was betrothed to. Her husband laid covered in the mist slowly lifting up as if lifting his blanket looking across calling. The still small voice seemed to beckon her.

"Come back home. Why did you leave my sons in a foreign land where they are strangers? Where the land is hostile. Bring them back to their father's land. Reunite them with their family." Each word struck on her heart strings, bringing back that mournful tune, causing streaming tears. She could hear the voice clearly.

Sobbing she said, "Honey, I am coming home now. I am sorry I left you so early."

The day's chores were disrupted. Her spirit was broken and needed nursing badly. The husband as well as her sons noticed her unhappy face and asked if she was sick. "No, I'm just tired." She looked pityingly at his sons and continued her task.

The father left them and went to check the old megapod nest for eggs for the evening meal. Mama Sandy called her sons over and told them her heart's hidden secret. "Mama, as you wish," they chorused.

That very afternoon they left for Kinona, their father's beloved village. The boys were happy Mama Sandy did the right thing, they will finally be home.

When they neared home, Sandy looked through her tear dimed eyes and said, "Your uncle, Anako is such a gifted singer and composer. Don't you ever forget that? It is through one of his songs that I have finally brought you back home, to where you belong."

Mama Won Twice

What is distance to her when love could cover all that? From Limki to Top Town and back. Isn't it anywhere near to walking from Kinona to Ivingoi or from Pindogori to Kinona? This is just peanuts. The only difference is that of the city's steamy climate. What is all the fuss when you have the 30t city bus service serving the route? 11A, 11B, 11C, 11D.

The morning ride to town was okay but the afternoon transport was a struggle. "You can't hop on the bus, if you aren't able to pay for the service." That leaves no option for Monica to walk from town to Eriku with her son through the National Botanical Garden, the shortest route for the first leg of the journey. It was indeed like the many forests they had been in back home, except that it was right in the heart of the city.

Tala excused himself from Monica, crawled into the undergrowth and then returned a few minutes later. Monica's motherly instincts told her to retrace her son's track. She returned with a neatly tied parcel of leaf resembling a mushroom pack back home. Tala soon realised what was going on and became embarrassed and protested. *Samting mi digim graun na haitim why yu kisim?* (I dug and hid it, why did you unearth it?)

"There is no need to protest, son. I did what I did for your safety. You know as well as I do that fearful *Masalai* lurk in *nambis* places." She spoke with such concern and urgency that Tala had to nod in agreement. "You won't go unpunished for trespassing and disturbance. They can make you sick and you know the rest of the story. I will make sure the green leafed parcel is finally dumped into the toilet!"

Like all mothers, she scolded her son. *"Yu wok moni bihain yu no inap tru long tingim mi long hat wok mi save mekim long yu. Bai yu amamas wantaim meri pikinini bilong yu."* (When you work in a paid job you won't remember and appreciate the many good things I did for you. It is all for your wife and kids). "Your brother would have said the same," Tala thought.

Tala was already making his way out of the Botanical Garden and was about to cross the road toward the Scout Hall when he thought of his mother. Turning he saw her trying her best to keep pace half running, half walking.

Together they crossed the road looking left and right for any approaching vehicles. Fortunately, the traffic wasn't busy.

The term two holiday was almost over and the Scout Hall was cramped with boys of Tala's age for practice. "Mama," said Tala, "I am privileged to be part of Buimo Road Pathfinder Club. These boys will be learning things not different to what we learn in Pathfinding."

"Hurry up or we'll have to walk all the way to Limki," Tala shouted over his shoulders to mama. He can't let mama walk with him this time.

"Uni gate, Uni gate, Uni gate!" the bus crew shouted as people crammed in to get a space. They ran to the door and got on. Mama sat at the doorway while Tala stood by the door. Mama was lucky as it was the last seat. People were racing to talk as they made themselves comfortable. Outside a bus was tooting its horn at full blast. The bus's way was being blocked by another one. "Get your bus moving, Kange!" shouted the angry crew.

"Hey! You?" The crew captured the passengers' attention. "You won't pay for the bus fare? Get out!" he said. Tala couldn't stand the eyes of the onlookers. Most paid no attention while others looked with pitying eyes. *"Mi tu bai go daun,"* said mama. *"No! Mama yu sidaun, boy tasol bai go daun,"* the crew said.

Seeing the pitying look on mama's face, the crew motioned Tala to go back in to where he was standing a while ago. Mama has won twice.

Going home towards Kamkumung, the car stereo went full blast, so that one could hardly hear passengers calling to stop at their destination. *"Draiva, yu orait oh! Daunim volume na harim long skel blong yu,"* shouted a mother from the middle row of seats. The others chorused after her, *"tru iyah!"*

For Tala he will barely forget this experience. "How much longer will this continue?" He thought. "May be with my goatee growing faster, I will be respected."

A Kid's Definition of Alcohol

Awateng and his family looked expectantly for the Bulolo PMVs at Lae Market's Raumai 18 shopping centre. *"Olgeta PMV blong Bulolo go pinis,"* someone from among the waiting passengers said. The last one left at 3:00pm. He cursed himself for not getting there on time.

But Awateng is a person who doesn't give up easily. He said a silent prayer and waited. That inner voice told him, there was still hope. He trusted his instincts and assured himself that they will still be going home.

His wife Gengasu turned and asked, "Are we still going home?"

"Of course we will," Awateng assured his wife. "But……." Gengasu was interrupted. "Bulolo, Bulolo," as the last PMV sped into the parking space. "That's Ali Bul Buang PMV," an excited passenger exclaimed.

Loaded soon, the PMV was heading home with excited passengers calling for the last stop at Freddy's store Snack Bar. Everyone got out to do their last shopping.

Awateng went into the Kai bar and bought 2 snack packs, flour balls and some soft drinks for the journey. When he came out the PMV wasn't there. Bewildered he tried to call his wife when a mother ran past him.

"Aiyo pikinini blong mi ya." She ran to the security guards for help crying. *"Pikinini blong mi PMV karim igo."* Confused she ran to whoever she could find, still crying. A baffled crowd gathered around her. Awateng approached the crowd and calmed the desperate, distraught mother.

He felt the buzz and he quickly reached into his pocket and brought out his Alcatel one touch Android phone. "Who could this be?" he thought.

"Hello honey? I was going to call you, but you rang. Where are you now? I'm still at Snack bar."

"Come to Morobe Stationary," and with that short message his wife ended the call.

Awateng directed the distraught mother across the road. "There she is, there she is!" everyone shouted. *"Nani pikinini blong yu krai na mipla painim yu ya."* What the lady didn't know was that the PMV was going to park at Morobe stationary and left the Snack Bar 2 minutes later.

Not long after and the PMV was heading home. A few more minutes and Ali Bul left the main Okuk Highway hitting the Bulolo section approaching Markham Bridge. The bridge is said to be the longest in the country although there is no record to prove this assumption. The afternoon breeze blew gently across Awateng's face. He enjoyed looking at the waterway downstream then across to Labu Butu. The river was dirty brown as usual but calm, resembling a tired and sleepy Waria tree python.

Awateng unzipped his backpack and removed the daily to read. The PMV was now running at high speed so that reading the newspaper was difficult. Peeping through the glass he saw the speedometer moving from 100 to 120. "That's fine," he thought, "We will reach Bulolo by 6pm passing the mighty Kumalu before dark."

He flipped quickly to the back page to see the NRL line up and other sports news. For the next one and a half hours he buried himself into the newspaper and devoured every page of it.

As they passed Timni village, the crew alerted the passengers for a quick stop at Gurako market to buy fresh garden produce and for a nature call.

At Gurako the passengers went out to buy their peanuts, kulau and other food stuff. After what seemed to be 30 minutes later, the driver started the PMV signalling that he was ready to continue the journey.

To everyone's amazement, Awateng's 2-year-old son yelled *"Daddy baim bia blong mi."* pointing in the direction of a vendor with a blue esky food cooler.

"Pikinini blong yu save dring bia?" an inquisitive mother queried.

"That's child abuse," another woman shot in.

"No, em i save kolim olgeta soft drinks beer," Awateng explained, perspiring. And he went on to further explain why he calls soft drinks beer.

Awateng's brothers are real humbugs. They try to ridicule Awateng's religious beliefs. He is a very faithful Seventh day Adventist Christian and doesn't take alcohol as well as other unclean food. They tell Awateng's son that Coca-Cola and other soft drinks are beer. That is how he started calling all soft drinks beer. The passengers laughed their hearts out.

When the Hunted Became the Hunter

The morning sun refused to come out early that day, as if suspecting imminent danger. It was so foggy and the grass was drenched wet. Rivers, streams and creeks were flooded, bursting their banks as a result of last night's torrential rain. The wet weather was a good augur for cassowary and pig hunting.

The hunters of the village gathered at Avundo's, the chief hunter's place. Yodelling could be heard from the village atop the hill and replies from down in the valley below as more and more men joined the hunting party.

For someone like Aputi, it was going to be his first. He got his bows and arrows and begged his father Yavita to go along. When he got permission to join the hunting party, he couldn't keep his excitement concealed but told his friends.

His friends begged their parents too, but not many were allowed to join the party. When the head hunter surveyed the group, he found a good team of mostly young men and five hunting dogs. They were all ready for the wild game with their bows and arrows. Only two had homemade guns, the chief hunter and a young man.

The party set out except for Yavita and his son Aputi. Yavita stayed back to fix his leaking roof before he could join them. Aputi grew impatient all the more. He cried and nagged his father to be fast. He worked as fast as he could and the task was completed in an hour's time. Finally, when everything was completed, they followed the hunting party.

As they emerged into the open grassy plain from the forest, they could hear a dog barking. The barking grew louder and louder as they approached the old garden patch.

Yavita warned his son to be vigilant as a wounded pig can use their last remaining strength to put down its foe and finish him off before it dies. He told him of an incident centuries ago in which a dying pig floored a hunter and ate him alive, leading to his eventual death as a result of blood loss.

Aputi was so afraid that he climbed a tree to watch from there. Yavita knew what to expect so he fixed his arrow to the bow ready to release it if the pig confronted him.

But the pig rushed at him from the thicket without a hint of warning. He lurched to the side, dropped everything and ran for his life to the safety of the nearby tree. Unfortunately, the tree could not hold his weight and swayed back and forth. It finally stood still when his weight balanced.

There was not a branch or anything that he could rest his feet on. He wished for the angry boar to go away so he could jump down.

Then he heard the pig munching away at something and turned to see. He couldn't believe what he saw. In the swine's mouth was raw human flesh dripping with blood. He felt warm gore running down his calf to the ankles. Looking down his leg he was taken aback to see a quarter of his calf muscle removed and part hanging lose. "Please help me, I'm a dead man", he sobbed his heart out in terror.

And when help finally came, they found the beast fallen dead under its victim. His kinsmen carried him to the nearest health facility.

He realised later how this had actually happened. When the tree bent backwards under his weight toward the angry boar, and before he could jerk his legs into a neat bundle, the pig got the chance there and then. So, it's either way; Go kill or get killed.

I Want to See It

One fine day in June 2022, a blue tinted 10-seater Toyota Land Cruiser was parked under the mango tree just outside the administration block. It was 9.00 am and the entire student body was in class. There was no one to attend to them. One of them stuck his head out of the window and spotted me at the rear end of the building.

I was checking my emails and WhatsApp messages as the Digicel signal strength was enough to go online. The person who spotted me walked over to me and greeted. "Hello Chaplain."

"Yes brother," I responded lifting my head up, "how may I help you?" So, this person knows me, I thought. He looked familiar. I searched my memory bank to ascertain where I met him before.

"We're a team from Bougainville Constitutional Planning Commission (BCPC), here to do awareness." That clicked me off to think of the Law & Justice sector awareness workshop a week before at Tsiroge conference centre near Bishop Wade Tarlena Secondary School. "If the Principal is around, could you inform him we're here?" he enquired. I left them there and went quickly to the office and informed the Principal.

After much discussion the Principal announced on the PA system that there was going to be a meeting in the Mess by both staff and students for an hour at lunch time with the BCPC personnel.

At lunch time the whole student body with staff members gathered to listen to the BCPC representatives. They briefly explained their reason for coming and asked for comments and questions.

There were hands going up from all corners of the room asking questions and making comments. One outstanding Kieta boy stood up and there was an uproar of laughter. Of course everyone knew who he was, and they watched and listened attentively to what he would say.

He was a problem child, a druggie. Even though he was a smart intelligent kid when he was first enrolled into Grade 9 the previous year, his marks nosedived after term 2 and continued into his final year at high school.

Although counselled, he couldn't give up on his habits easily. He struggled to study hard, but his addictions interfered with his education.

Here he was trying to give his views. "You are so much concerned about political independence, but my school does not have a basketball court and other sporting facilities," he confidently said. Everyone once more roared into laughter.

"Yes young man, that is a valid question," responded the team leader. "To answer your question I would say that PNG got her Independence in 1975 without much infrastructure and that is the path we're taking."

I turned around to see if he was there listening. And to my surprise I saw him disappearing into the Grade 10 boys' dormitory. I wished he was there to listen to the response by himself. The bell rang for period 8. As a matter of courtesy, the Principal thanked them for coming and they left for Buka.

I left the hall and headed home. My house was near the boys' dorm and I thought of checking up on the boys before going to my house.

I saw the young man coming out of the dorm just in time. "Young man, you asked a very important question today, but you were not there to listen to the response made," I said jokingly.

He gave an intelligent answer. *"Mi no laik harim tasol mi laik lukim samting"*. (I don't want to listen to sweet talks but see tangible results.) I never expected him to make such a calculated comment.

"POETRY IS THE SPONTANEOUS OVERFLOW OF POWERFUL FEELINGS: IT TAKES ITS ORIGIN FROM EMOTION RECOLLECTED IN TRANQUILITY."

William Wordsword

Sonoma Race - 2016 November

Brothers all are we
  We sailed the ship together
Thrown overboard within an inch of sighting land
  Struggling to keep afloat
Waves of all sizes break over me
  Faced with all dangers, scary, dreary sea monsters
I try to get me into the boat
  Putting up with the rolling sea
The tempest raging and the bellows tossing high
  Often times riding the crest of the waves or being run over
Being swallowed and vomited
  The sky is overshadowed with blackness, no shelter or help is near
My friends look to me with pitying eyes
  Cannot help but offer a prayer of consolation
Say a word of encouragement, shed tears
  The ship sails to shore without me
And finally berths into hangar
  I watch with a heavy heart, tossed here and there
Friends who made it safely shout for joy
  Hip, hip hooray!
Tears of joy flood their eyes
  Looking back they see the struggles
Sea sickness and the ever-present dangers of the sea
  They grab their luggage and go their own way
They turn back, look at me
  Encourage me to continue to keep afloat and wait for the next passenger vessel.

Gone are the Days

Gone are the days
  When the moons were endless
Only the sun and moon could tell
  Moons had no names
They were only known by seasons
  Gone are the days
When the days and nights were long
  Time enough for all daily chores
Gone are the days
  When time was ours
Grandfather and his sons could complete the day's work
  Story time in the house tambaran for men and boys
Gone are the days
  When time could not be borrowed
Mothers and girls completed gardening
  Ladies spend leisure time gossiping
Today we have the machine
  We can count months
Months have names
  But moons are shorter
We bargain for time
  We borrow time.

What Meets the Eye is Deceptive

What I see is the colour
Not the person
What I see is the deed
Not the person
What I see is gender
Not the person
What meets the eye is deceptive

He is a drug fanatic
She is a prostitute
He is a HIV AIDS carrier
She is illiterate
He is disabled
What meets the eye is deceptive

He is educated
She is working
He is a Christian
She is an agnostic
What meets the eye is deceptive

He is from Wabag
She is from Sepik
He is from Goilala
She is from Chimbu
What meets the eye is deceptive

But bear in mind
He is God's creation
She is God's image
See them as God's creation
Not as what I see
See and value them
From God's perspective

Not status, prestige, gender or colour
Not the head content
Not the house content
But the HEART content
For what meets the eye is deceptive.

The Other Side of the Day

When the world goes into a deep slumber
  The misty mountain village
Sits atop lonely covered in white sheets
  Cold from the frozen air
Shivering from this bone chilling cold
  Activities ceased yesterday
With the fast evaporation of the daylight hours
  Quietness takes over
The Hussle and bustle of the day
  And this part of the day is for no human
Ruled by the tewels, masalais and other nocturnals
  They have gone, the cuscus hunters
They know where to find the kapuls
  The signs are evident, droppings and bark chewing
Towards the edge of the day
  The hunter returns with their trophies
Drunk with sleep
  Drops on the bed and he's gone.

Father's Death

Oh papa, why leave so early
  You told me that you would come to see me
I sent you money

But you said, *"Mi planim gaden pastaim"*
I called to remind you
　You said, *"Mama em wanpela so wet liklik"*
So I waited

When the phone rang I eagerly picked it up
　Knowing that you were calling to let me know you were coming
But Mama's cries greeted me instead
　She said, *"Papa bilong yu i lusim yumi pinis"*
This rent and tore my heart

The whole world came tumbling down
　Its weight unbearable
Am I dreaming? Realization of the truth otherwise
　Tears freely fell

Precious moments cherished and missed
　Recollecting missed opportunities and joyous moments together
The huge shade tree that provided shade
　Came crushing down leaving no part intact. I could feel it
You can see it What can you and I do? Regret sets in

When evening shadows fall
　Crying and weeping
The morrow will dawn upon my sorrow
You left one thing
　A photograph of yourself in my heart album
Twenty years between us
　Has distorted your picture but memory lasts forever.

Be free bury the past

I see you a human
  I see you a family member
I see you a brother
  While you see me differently

You are still fearful of me
  You still carry the past with you
I have buried your past
  Even though I still have the scar you created

Just let the past in its resting place
  Don't go back to visit it
And cry over the grave

I know it haunts you
  But it is no longer alive
I have buried mine

  Bury yours
Come breathe in the fresh air
  And enjoy the sunshine
Enjoy the once lost brotherly love.

Black But Beautiful

Beauty is not confined to colour
  Cats only see some colours
You judge by the colour
  You ignore the black
Yet this colour is beautiful
  Beauty is nothing to do with the colour
Painted black but beautiful
  See the red, black and gold with the streak of white
Flying above
  Isn't that beautiful?
Being one of the many different colours that decorates this world.
  Black is just another colour
Colour is not value
  What lies beneath is
Ugliness is not confined to black
  But it's just being different
Being unique
  Bougainville, black but beautiful.

No Real Black Man

Real black man did not come from Africa
  Nor from Asia
They are not black Americans or Europeans either
  They are not the Pacific Islanders
The real black man is one
  -who kills his fellow man
  -who creates dangerous weapons of destruction
  -who is against humanity
Because his heart is black, real black.

The Thief

Look around, peep, peep
  Front, back, side to side
    Nobody's around
      Nobody's watching
Move now
  Quietly, tip toe, tip toe
    Don't worry about the "thumb, thumb inside.
    Easy, easy, no noise
Grab it, take it easy
  You're alone
    NOW RUN! Fast, faster, fast, faster
      Slow down
Stop, you're out of reach
  Now at your command.

The New Moon

Last night I saw the moon coming
  It has just woken up from its sleeping chamber, the sea
Later I saw it underneath the black tree
  Minutes later I saw it climbing the tree
It reached the top in a few minutes
  As I wasn't watching, it left the tree for the snowy mountains
It scaled the mountains as an expert mountaineer
  Sometimes absorbed into the vegetation
Appearing randomly to take a breather
  Then reached the mountaintop very quickly
Now competing for the floating space in the starry sky.

Malaria Attack

Aiyo, Aiya
  Mama iyo-o-o
My head, my head
  Oh my head
This must be another attack of malaria
  Kisim anali, rausim blut nogut
Get the *salat*, apply to the head
  Aiyo mama, inap ya. Stop the pain
It's killing me.

Widening Gap

1960s, 70s and 80s
  Many left the village
For lack of services
  In search of employment
In fear of sorcery
  Home was very sweet and compelling
A formidable community
  The urge to go back home was very high

In the wake of the 1990s
  They left the village
For lack of services
  In search of employment and life's opportunities
In fear of sorcery
  Home was sweet and compelling
The urge to go back was high

In the Rush hours of the 2000
  Masses flee
In fear of the GUN
  The super power
Home is good but not inviting
  No urge to go back
The heart bleeds in silence
  No sweet home instead bitterness.

I'd Rather Shut My Mouth

This wouldn't have happened if I didn't tell her
  I'd rather keep my mouth shut
Because I whispered, there are more uninvited guests
  I'd rather keep my mouth shut
Because I informed him, he beat his wife very badly.
  I'd rather keep my mouth shut
My words backfired at me
  I'd rather keep my mouth shut
Because of my double tongue
  My friend deserted me
I'd rather keep my mouth shut
  Police interrogated me for being an informer
I'd rather keep my mouth shut
  I am hated because of my own words
I'd rather keep my mouth shut
  He died because of my words
I'd rather keep my mouth shut.

Blame or Accept

From time behind the recorded past
  From behind the time curtain
To the recent past
  Within the pen's reach
Family ties were strong
  Bound together in cords of iron
Communalism rooted in kinship resulted in tribal unity
  Every one lived next door to each other
Where they could hear each other
  Where they could console each other
And live for each other

Picking up from yesterday
  All ties are fast deteriorating.
Communalism is suffering
  Blood connections live thousands of miles apart
Where they cannot hear each other
  Where they cannot console each other
Or live for each other

The oldies try their best to connect the past with the present
  They are the last strap in this time cord
When they pass on they create a gully impassable.

All in One, One in All

He wears his father's face
  Attached with his mother's nose
Possess his mother's temperament
  Has his father's intelligence
Sits like his paternal grandfather
  Walks like his maternal grandfather
Works like his paternal grandmother
  Eats like his maternal grandmother
A quarter of the father
  A quarter of the mother
And half of the grandparents.

Who Cares?

I don't care how you sit there
  As long as you get to your destination.
Whether you sit or stand
  Whether seats are available or not
I don't care whether you reach your destination on time
  As long as you get there.
I don't care whether you have urgent work to do in town.
  As long as the sun is still up there.

The Dotted Sky

At twilight the sky is dotted black
   Staining the white veil
Spread in all directions
   Beyond the power of the detergent
To bleach to snow white
   Visual as a fly, even a pencil dot
Moving northward
   Destination unknown
Starting in the south
   Place of origin unknown
A common sight every day
   The return journey?
Don't ask me because I don't know
   I only see them moving in the same direction
They are the foxes who can fly
   And not the barking pet foxes
But the flying foxes of Bougainville.

The Provoking Insect

It landed without me knowing
  Minutes later felt an itch
Turned to see a winged insect
  Tummy red as a bird eye-chilly
As I raised my hand to kill it
  It flew away
Leaving me with anger and frustration
  For not accomplishing the task
Is so infuriating than the sight of it
  I see it go and disappears thin
Try to follow but too smart
  The surrounding absorbs it
Anger and frustration make me swear
  If you were as big as a grasshopper
I will squeeze you leaving no trace.

The Hunter's Wish

Kalando nemba, Kalando nemba[7]
  My dog, my dog
Sniff here, sniff there
  For both the 4 legged and the 2 legged
The pig or better a cassowary
  The possum or better a fowl
The cuscus or better a pigeon.
  I am in the communal hunting ground.
Nagaria[8] head waters
  Live these black 4 legged creatures
In the hollow of the trees
  But you seem to sniff the air
You have given me nothing now
  That I will go home empty handed
No protein on the table
  For me and my household
We will eat *kaukau* and that's it
  And the water used in boiling them
To wash it down.

---

7. Fore language Okapa meaning 'my dog'
8. Name of a creek in my area

Sacred Exposed

Wrapped in grass skirts down to the feet
  Covered in leaves and bilum from the shoulders to the waist line
Virginity was protected

She was the real woman
  Sought after by the real man
For she was the best woman
  For the best man he was

She revealed her breasts to feed
  She uncovered herself in front her husband.
From skirt to trousers
  From meri blouse to open necked shirts.
From being a woman to a man
  She walks like a man.

And in bedroom clothes she adorns herself.
  In revealing outfits she clothes
Exposing her sacredness.
  The breast is now bare
Lose bums reveals the inner cloth
  The UP[9] is seen which was concealed
A taboo broken

---
9. UP - underpants

The rich gold deposits
Are exposed
They are up for grabs
It attracts flies
It's anybody's
There's no use for retaliation
There's no use taking someone to court.
Over rape and sexual exploitation
Because it has become a public property.
And no longer a sole property.

Light as a feather

I climb up the tree
    And the wind blows me down
Because I am light as a feather
    I hit my back
And I say.......
    Oh my back
And where is my bone.

He is Coming Soon

I see the night sky is different tonight
      Different than usual
I'm unconscious to what others are seeing
      Can't you see the sky is changing?
Everybody see the moon lit sky
      They love to sit up and gossip
Without seeing what I see
      I can see and hear
Silence is broken for there is singing up in heaven
      I see the sky brighten up
Unspeakable, incomprehensible
      There is no dark valley here below
I see my king and saviour Jesus Christ
      Coming in the clouds, the clouds of heaven, the eastern sky
Hallelujah! Praise the Lord
      With great power and glory
And His angels accompanying Him
      The sky is full of them
I can hear the Angel calling out my name
      In a crystal clear melodious voice
Look up high and see your master is coming for you
      Yes one of these days I am going home
Where no sorrows and heartaches attends.

God Created the Sun

God created the sun through the Son
 For to serve its purpose but man worships the sun instead of the Son
Sun of righteousness instead of the sun
 The sun obeyed when the son of man Joshua commanded and it stood still
The sun stopped shining when the only Son of GOD hung dying on the cross
 The sun obeyed the Son, the created respected its creator
Natural man harness the sun's energy to produce solar power
 Spiritual man accepts the Son to produce light which glorifies the Father who is in heaven
Old Jerusalem needs the sun
 New Jerusalem will need the Son
The fallen earth depends on the sun for survival
 The earth made new will depend on the Son for all its needs.

Time

Time, time, time, oh time
    How much do I need you?
You are precious
    Everyone has the same amount of time.
The gardener, the professional, the student, the business man
    To the business man, time is money
To the professional time is money, time is promotion
    To the students time is education
To me it can't be bought, Nor can it be saved
    Money is not time either
Time is precious
    Time is life I can't afford to lose
I regret misusing and abuse of time
    Many people don't see the beauty of time.
They don't value it until it catches up on them.

Mama's Silent Tears

She was really suffering
    Suffering from the pain she carried inside
The pain that didn't go away
    The pain that bothered her all along
She shed silent tears

Take me to the Clinic
    She would say
Spare a moment to accompany me to the hospital
    I am sick you cannot see
Only she could feel the magnitude of the pain
    Mama shed silent tears

She appeared healthy
    She went on with her daily chores
Cooking, washing, marketing and gardening
    She complained of her condition
But drowned with her love for the family
    Put her back to work
She shed silent tears

She gave a faked smile in front of people
      Just to conceal her predicament
Mama shed silent tears

Mama was a strong spirited woman
      A courageous woman
She stood by her husband
      To put food on the table
To help pay her children's school fees
      But she wept in silence

Now that mama's gone
      Regret is inevitable for the missed opportunities
It saddens me to realize the fact
      She is gone, gone forever
It pains me to think of those moments
      I should have done this
I should have done that.

Love Thief

Love between couples
  Is love that came from the creator's hand.
Is love that is protected by the marriage sanctity.
  Is love that survives isolation
Is love that knows no end.
  This is the definition of true love
Genuine love is…..
  For the adult he and the adult she
To be cherished
  Not for the young he and the young she
To be abused
  The thief comes in
Very attractive for even the faithful
  He is not seductive
But entices
  The lure is money
The lure is a car
  The lure is position
Money and possessions are the culprits
  They are the thieves
Thieves of true love.

The Lost Fisherman's Fear

The day when the Ocean met the sky
    It was love at first sight
The green floating ball
    And the gigantic blue canvas
When the fisherman lost his way
    He looked in all directions
They were the same
    Looking beyond the flat still surface
Nothing but blackness
    Eerie Dreary atmosphere
This raises goose bumps
    Atmosphere around is alive
Full of them
    The sea monsters have already tasted me
They have already torn me to pieces
    I am but the fishes' food.

No One is Listening

Hunger drives me to speak in terms immeasurable
  It drives me to act immorally
No one is listening

I groan because I am sick
  There are no drugs at the clinic
Mother is in anguish from breech birth
  Message for help is sent while she dies waiting.
No one is listening

I cry out in pain from social ills
  Schools are suspended because no supplies are coming
My son is growing old without an education
  Roads have deteriorated
No road services
  My back is aching
Carrying coffee bags
  I become a human camel
No one is listening

I am bullied by the privileged
  It costs much to match up
My earnings and even my life

I am suppressed by the Asian business man
I cry out for deliverance
  No one is listening

The men in blue shoot at me
  To defend the China man because he has money
And kills one of his own for no reason
  His death speaks volumes
No one is listening

Brian Kramer is speaking his heart out
  Others are muted
Gerry Juffa is talking sense
  Kerenga Kua is giving words of wisdom
John Momis is shouting his concern
  Mekere Morauta is telling the truth
No one is listening

Sons and daughters of this land
  Shout again for the whole world to hear.

My Lae

Lae oh Lae, Lae of yesteryears
   The Lae my father knew of
And the Lae I came to love and grew fond of
   The Lae I came to see as my home

When a visitor, father slept on the streets
   Sharing the night with stray dogs and cats
But he was not alone
   His brothers from other provinces slept 5 yards

He walked from Limki to Eriku in search of a job
   He walked from 4 mile to top Town in search of a living
He walked from Bumayong to Market in search of employment
   Walked back at sundown to retire for the night

Years have gone by and Lae,
   My Lae has since changed
From Wopa country to Rainy Lae
   From beautiful green Lae to Pot hole city
From Kumul blong Morobe to thug infested Lae
   Street mangis rule the streets
Pickpockets rule the bus tops
   Fear has ruled the hearts of the people

Lae oh my Lae, You are changing
Your colour is fading
Give me back my Lae.

Comrades

The colour didn't matter
    Nor was the age difference
Gender wasn't a barrier either
    We were comrades

We had a common enemy
    We fought together
Back to back we defended our territory
    We cried together
We shed tears together
    We had a common goal
We were real comrades

We prayed together, petitioning our heavenly father
    We shared our problems together
We leaned on each other
    We consoled each other
When I fell down you picked me up
    When you fell down I picked you up
We were comrades

But time has come that you must hang your boots
    As comrades we must say goodbye
Knowing that God will go with you
    With a heavy heart I let you go
Now I have to find new comrades to continue this life
    When you finally come to the end of your life journey
Your wish will be granted
    We will honour you by burying you in your military uniform.